MAPLE SYRUP

ELAINE ELLIOT

Photographed on location by Julian Beveridge

FORMAC PUBLISHING COMPANY LIMITED
HALIFAX 1998

PHOTO CREDITS:
All photography by Julian Beveridge, except where noted below:
Nova Scotia Dept. of Agriculture and Marketing: p.4; p 5, bottom; p. 6, bottom; p. 9, bottom.
New Brunswick Forest Extension Service: p 6, top. Ontario Ministry of Agriculture and Food: p. 5, top; p. 8, top. Vermont Travel Division: p. 7, top & bottom; p. 8, bottom. Canadian Tourism Commission: p. 9, top. E. Kedl: p. 30; p. 57; p. 59; p. 63.

PARTICIPATING ESTABLISHMENTS:

A. Hiram Walker Estate Heritage Inn, St. Andrews, NB

The Algonquin Hotel, St. Andrews, NB

Aux Anciens Canadiens, Quebec City, Que

Bluenose Lodge, Lunenburg, NS

The Briar Inn and Country Club, Jackson's Point, Ont

Carriage House Inn, Fredericton, NB

Catherine McKinnon's Spot O' Tea, Stanley Bridge, PEI

Château Beauvallon, Mt. Tremblant, Que

Château Bonne Entente, Sainte Foy, Que

The Dundee Arms, Charlottetown, PEI

Falcourt Inn, Nictaux, NS

Grandview Inn, Huntsville, Ont

Hotel Beausejour, Moncton, NB

Inn at Thorn Hill, Jackson, NH

Inn on the Lake, Waverley, NS

Keltic Lodge, Ingonish, NS

Liscombe Lodge, Liscomb Mills, NS

Loon Bay Lodge, St. Stephen, NB

Manoir Victoria, Quebec City, Que

Murray Manor Bed and Breakfast, Yarmouth, NS

The Palliser Restaurant, Truro, NS

The Parker's Lodge, Val-David, Que

Planters' Barracks Country Inn, Starrs Point, NS

The Prince Edward Hotel, Charlottetown, PEI

The Quaco Inn, St. Martins, NB

Seasons in Thyme, Summerside, PEI

Shaw's Hotel, Brackley Beach, PEI

Stonehurst Manor, North Conway, NH

Sugarbush Inn, Warren, Vt

Unni's Restaurant, Halifax, NS

Wickwire House Bed and Breakfast, Kentville, NS

Dedication:

This book is dedicated to my husband Robert and our sons, thanking them for their continued encouragement and support.

Formac Publishing Company Limited acknowledges the support of the Department of Canadian Heritage and the Nova Scotia Department of Education and Culture in the development of writing and publishing in Canada.

Canadian Cataloguing in Publication Data
Elliot, Elaine, 1939-
    Maple syrup
    (Maritime flavours)
    ISBN 0-88780-420-9

1. Cookery (Maple sugar and syrup). 2. Maple syrup. I. Beveridge, Julian. II. Title. III. Series.

TX767.M3E56 1998   641.6'364   C97-950242-X

Formac Publishing Company Limited
5502 Atlantic Street
Halifax, N.S.
B3H 1G4

Distribution in the United States:
Seven Hills Book Distributors
49 Central Avenue
Cincinnati, OH 45202

CONTENTS

INTRODUCTION

aple syrup is so much more than a
pancake, waffle or ice cream topping. It is a delicacy produced in Atlantic Canada,
Ontario, Quebec and New England, which the chefs of the many inns and
restaurants of the "maple regions" are familiar with. They have been more than
generous in sharing their breakfast, main course entrées, and, of course, dessert
recipes. In these pages you will find their best dishes, from a Prince Edward Island
inn's Pan Roasted Pork Tenderloin to a New Hampshire inn's Corn Meal and
Bacon Pancakes, along with some typical Québécois *l'érable cuisine* and an
innovative Maritime chef's maple-infused fettucini. The recipes have been tested
and adjusted for "at-home cooks" for four to six servings.

Fine food presentation is an art, one which is receiving increased emphasis by
chefs everywhere. Most of the dishes photographed in this book were captured on
site — what better way to show how these recipes are presented by their originators!

Affectionately called "Queen of the Forests," the sugar, hard or rock maples are botanically known as *acer saccharum*. Found in eastern North America, their range extends from Newfoundland, the Maritimes and New England, through Quebec and Ontario to Manitoba and southward into Kansas. These giants tower in the forests, a mature tree the leaves turn a dazzling red, deep orange or brilliant gold. Like a wave spreading on the shore, this colourful display moves from the north of the range, in Quebec and Ontario, southward through the Maritimes and New England.

The sheer beauty of this seasonal phenomenon has made October and early

Maples put on a colourful autumn display

growing to heights of 30 metres with a girth of up to 4 metres. Away from the confines of other trees, their giant green-leafed branches fill out and spread, making them into beautiful shade trees in parks and gardens.

In autumn, however, the maples stand out from the crowd. Triggered by shorter days and cooler nights, the cells in the leaves shut off their natural flow of chlorophyll, and November a prime travel time, extending the tourist season to the benefit of those involved in the innkeeping trade. Then, with the falling of the last leaves, these giant trees lie dormant, slumbering through the long eastern winter.

The tree's ability to provide sap is the feature that concerns us here. Harvesting the clear liquid, and "sugaring," as the process of rendering syrup and sugar from

Plastic piping, a sign of the times in this Nova Scotia maple grove

Mild March days get the sap running in this New Brunswick maple grove

sap is called, can only begin when the maples awaken after winter to the gentler temperatures of spring. The warm sun falling upon their uppermost twigs sends signals to the roots; the sugar and water stored there for the winter then slide up the trunk to provide nutrients for the branches above. At night, when the temperature drops below freezing,

the sap runs back down the trunk into the root system. Ideal sugaring conditions may begin in early March when daytime temperatures are in the 5°C range, dipping to around -4°C at night. A good season lasts until mid-April. A successful sugaring season requires this variation of temperatures so that the sap will run freely.

How does this clear watery liquid become the acclaimed maple syrup and sugar? In earlier times, the "sugarer" hung small pails from spigots placed in the trunks of the sugar maples. The pails were emptied every few days into vats which were hauled by horse and sleigh to a sugaring hut. In a typical "Currier and Ives" setting, the vats of sap would then simmer away on woodburning stoves in the "sugar huts". This was, indeed, a regular part of the year's cycle for early North American farmers. Each season, they produced maple syrup for their own use and for the market. It was the first crop of the year.

Sap from hundreds of trees feeds into a Vermont sugar shack

Strict regulations govern the industry on both sides of the border. Equipment must be kept scrupulously clean, the highly perishable sap must be boiled as soon as it is gathered and the process controlled by the use of reliable hydrometers and thermometers. To replace the old fashioned chore of hauling sap to the sugar shack for processing, today's syrup makers have miles of plastic tubing that carry the pumped sap to large evaporators. Under the watchful eye of the "boiler," the syrup will be taken off at just the right moment, strained and bottled in sterilized containers. Maple syrup is marketed in glass, plastic or metal containers. However, some producers prefer glass bottles because they feel that extended storage in metal or plastic may cause the syrup to change flavour.

The departments of agriculture in both Canada and the United States enforce strict grading rules, and the syrup producers use the Lovibond Grading Kit which offers a series of standardized colours to establish the grade of their product. In Canada, premium syrup is graded as Canada #1 extra light and medium; also available is Canada #2 amber, which is darker in colour and has a stronger flavour. Purists feel that the stronger flavoured syrups are ideal for cooking and baking. In most

Mass production has changed the face of maple syrup production and today's successful "sugarer" must have a knowledge of his tree stand, and be willing to invest in equipment and promotion. To produce a marketable quantity of syrup, hundreds of trees must be tapped. A large tree may accommodate up to three small drill holes or taps, each producing 30 to 40 gallons of sap per season, which will condense into only 3 to 4 quarts of syrup.

"Sugaring off"

Visitors to an Ontario sugar shack make a close inspection of a modern evaporator

produced, including maple cream or butter, maple candy, and maple sugar. Maple cream, which is sold in plastic tubs, is a soft spread made by heating finished maple syrup to 113°C, then cooling it to 21°C and whipping to incorporate air into the thickened mass. Maple candy is made by heating syrup to a temperature of 113°C and then cooling to 68°C, before pouring it into candy molds. Maple sugar, the result of continuing to boil down the syrup until almost all liquid has evaporated, is about twice as sweet as granulated sugar and imparts a wonderful maple flavour when used to sweeten drinks or baked goods.

states the United States Department of Agriculture grades syrup as Grade A or "fancy," with syrups ranging from light amber to medium amber. U. S. Grade B is a dark amber syrup with a hearty flavour and deemed very suitable for cooking. It is generally felt that the mid-range syrups have the most robust flavour.

Various maple confections are also

Pure maple syrup may be stored in the freezer for over a year. Unopened containers should be stored in a cool, dry place for up to three or four months, but must be stored in a refrigerator once opened.

Pure maple syrup contains no preservatives, artificial colours or flavourings. It is a natural sweetener, full of natural sugars

A "boiler" keeps a close eye on the evaporation process

Waiting for goodies at a "sugarbush restaurant" in Québec

and nutrients. A 1/4 cup serving provides approximately 206 calories.

It is important to remember that only products marked "pure maple syrup" are truly maple syrup. Table syrups, pancake syrups and maple-flavoured syrups are not pure maple syrup and cannot be substituted for ingredients in these recipes.

The origin of maple harvesting is without written record and historians are not in agreement as to who first perfected the art of producing this golden delight. Folk lore and oral history tells us that Native Americans living along the eastern seaboard taught the European settlers how to obtain this marvellous and nutritious syrup. To them, we are eternally grateful. May you enjoy the recipes.

Maple snow candy is a natural hit

BREAKFAST OR BRUNCH

*I*f you think Maple Syrup is simply a pancake topper, think again! In this section there are a number of breakfast or brunch options, all using pure maple syrup!

◄ *Peerless Cranberry Maple Sugar Scones are served up at the Wickwire House Bed and Breakfast*

PEERLESS CRANBERRY MAPLE SUGAR SCONES

WICKWIRE HOUSE BED AND BREAKFAST, KENTVILLE, NS

Maple sugar, which is about twice as sweet as white sugar, is made by continuing to boil down the maple sap until the liquid has almost completely evaporated. At Wickwire House, the scones are served with jam or English Double Devon Cream.

1 1/2 cups flour

1/4 cup maple sugar

1 teaspoon baking powder

1/4 teaspoon salt

1/4 teaspoon baking soda

1/3 cup dried cranberries

grated zest of 1 orange

1/3 cup butter

1/2 cup sour cream

1–2 tablespoons maple sugar (second amount)

Preheat oven to 400°F. In a mixing bowl combine flour, maple sugar, baking powder, salt, and baking soda. Stir in dried cranberries and orange zest. Cut in butter until mixture resembles coarse crumbs, stir in sour cream. Shape dough into a ball and pat into an 8-inch round on a lightly greased cookie sheet. Cut dough into eight wedges and sprinkle with additional maple sugar. Bake 18 to 20 minutes or until lightly browned. Yield 8 wedges.

SMOKED BREAKFAST SAUSAGES WITH MAPLE APPLE GLAZE

A. HIRAM WALKER ESTATE HERITAGE INN, ST. ANDREWS, NB

This is an excellent brunch dish that can be prepared in advance and served at the table in a chafing dish. Innkeeper Elizabeth Cooney uses a combination of Red Delicious and Granny Smith apples to provide colour contrast and serves the dish accompanied by scrambled eggs and seasonal fruit.

8–12 small pork sausages

1/3 cup butter

1/4 cup pecan halves

2 tart apples, sliced (Red Delicious & Granny Smith)

1/4 teaspoon cinnamon

generous grating of fresh nutmeg

1/2 cup pure maple syrup

Pierce sausages, then parboil them for 5 minutes to remove excess fat. Drain and set aside. Melt butter in a large sauté pan, stir in pecans, apple slices, cinnamon, nutmeg, and maple syrup. Add sausages, bring to a simmer and cook, stirring frequently until apples are barely tender. Serve with scrambled eggs. Serves 4.

Picture-perfect Smoked Breakfast Sausages with Maple Apple Glaze ▶

FRENCH TOAST STUFFED WITH MAPLE GLAZED APPLES

A. HIRAM WALKER ESTATE HERITAGE INN, ST. ANDREWS, NB

Elizabeth Cooney, innkeeper of the A. Hiram Walker Estate Heritage Inn incorporates maple syrup into many of her breakfast dishes. She tells me that this recipe is equally delicious if you substitute fresh peach slices for the apples.

6-8 slices fresh homemade bread, each 2 inches thick

1/2 cup light cream

4 eggs, beaten

1/2 cup butter

1/4 cup pecans

2 tart apples, pared and cut in small slices

1/4 teaspoon cinnamon

1/4 cup pure maple syrup

freshly ground nutmeg

2 tablespoons butter, second amount

Preheat oven to 150°F. Slice bread, then cut a pocket almost all the way through the bread and set aside. In a bowl combine cream and eggs.

Melt butter in a large skillet, stir in pecans, apple slices, cinnamon, maple syrup and a generous grating of fresh nutmeg. Bring to a simmer and cook, stirring frequently until apples are barely tender. Remove from heat.

In a large skillet, over medium heat, melt second amount of butter. Dip one slice of bread at a time in egg mixture, pressing down to allow eggs to soak through. Lift out, allowing excess egg mixture to drip back into the bowl. Fry the soaked bread until golden brown, on one side only, approximately 2 minutes. Carefully open pocket and spoon in a small amount of the pecan mixture. Flip bread and brown other side, repeating procedure and adding more butter if necessary. Keep toast warm in a 150°F oven and serve with additional maple syrup and seasonal fruit. Serves 4–6.

◄ *Innkeeper Elizabeth Cooney's French Toast Stuffed with Maple Glazed Apples*

CORN MEAL AND BACON PANCAKES

STONEHURST MANOR,
NORTH CONWAY, NH

Nestled in a pine forest, Stonehurst Manor is what everyone dreams of as a classic New England Inn. To further fulfil such expectations the chef proudly serves elegant meals with a local flavour.

2 strips bacon, fried crisp and crumbled

1/3 cup yellow corn meal

1 cup flour

1 teaspoon salt

2 teaspoons baking powder

1 egg

1 1/4 cups milk

1 tablespoon bacon fat

pure maple syrup for topping

Fry bacon until crisp, then crumble, reserving 1 tablespoon of the bacon fat. Mix together the corn meal, flour, salt and baking powder. In a separate bowl, whisk together the egg, milk and bacon fat. Stir this mixture slowly into the dry ingredients, mixing well. The batter should be fairly thin, so you may add a little more milk if necessary. Stir in the crumbled bacon. Cook pancakes in a greased skillet and serve with butter and pure maple syrup. Serves 4.

GRILLED HAM SLICES WITH MAPLE GLAZE

A. HIRAM WALKER ESTATE HERITAGE INN, ST. ANDREWS, NB

Innkeeper Elizabeth Cooney marinates her breakfast ham slices overnight in maple syrup. The result is subtle, yet oh so delicious.

Uncooked ham slice, approximately 16 ounces

6–8 whole cloves

1/2 cup pure maple syrup

6–8 eggs, scrambled

The evening before serving, stud the fatty edge of the ham slice with whole cloves and place in a shallow glass container. Pour maple syrup over ham, cover with plastic wrap and allow to marinate in the refrigerator until breakfast time.

To serve, lift ham from syrup and grill until cooked through and lightly browned on both sides, approximately 8 minutes. Prepare scrambled eggs while ham is cooking and serve with ham. Serves 4.

CAPE SMOKEY BLUEBERRY PANCAKES

KELTIC LODGE, INGONISH, NS

The chef at Keltic prides himself in using local produce. He serves his pancakes topped with pure maple syrup from the annual sugaring harvest.

2 eggs

1/4 cup vegetable oil

1/4 cup honey

2/3 cup plain yoghurt

1/2 cup milk

1/2 cup sweet apple cider or juice

1 2/3 cups flour

1/2 teaspoon salt

1 1/2 teaspoon baking soda

1/2 teaspoon cinnamon

fresh or frozen blueberries

pure maple syrup

Beat eggs in a large bowl. Add oil, honey, yoghurt, milk and cider and beat well. Mix together flour, salt, baking soda and cinnamon. Add flour mixture to yoghurt mixture, stirring only until combined.

Preheat a greased skillet to 400°F. Spoon a small amount of batter on skillet, sprinkle with blueberries and when bubbles form on uncooked side of pancakes, flip and continue cooking until done. Serve with butter and pure maple syrup. Serves 4–6.

TINY SCOTTISH PANCAKES WITH BRANDIED MAPLE SYRUP

THE MURRAY MANOR BED AND BREAKFAST, YARMOUTH, NS

Joan Semple of the Murray Manor serves these tiny pancakes accompanied by pure maple syrup infused with a wee dram of brandy.

2 eggs

1/2 cup sugar

1 teaspoon vanilla

1 cup milk

1 1/2 cups flour

1 tablespoon baking powder

1/4 teaspoon salt

1 tablespoon butter, melted

1/2 cup blueberries

oil for browning, as necessary

3/4 cup pure maple syrup

2 tablespoons brandy

Preheat a griddle to 375°F. In a large mixing bowl combine eggs, sugar, vanilla, and milk. In a separate bowl sift together the flour, baking powder, and salt. Add flour mixture to egg mixture, mixing only until blended. Stir in melted butter and blueberries.

Pour approximately 1 tablespoon of batter onto the griddle for each pancake. As small bubbles appear on the top, turn and brown the other side. Combine pure maple syrup and brandy in a small pitcher and serve over pancakes. Yields 20–24 small pancakes.

WICKWIRE HOUSE MAPLE PECAN BANANA PANCAKES

WICKWIRE HOUSE BED AND BREAKFAST, KENTVILLE, NS

Innkeepers Darlene and Jim Peerless advise that "Maple caresse" fresh cheese is available in the yogurt section of most supermarkets. They toast their pecans by sprinkling them on a cookie sheet and baking in a moderate oven for 2–3 minutes.

2 extra large eggs

2 cups buttermilk

2 cups mashed bananas

1/4 cup maple syrup

1/4 cup vegetable oil

2 1/4 cups flour

1 tablespoon baking powder

1 teaspoon soda

1/4 teaspoon salt

1 cup chopped pecans, toasted

3 medium bananas, sliced

3 cups fresh strawberry halves

"Maple caresse" fresh cheese

maple syrup

Beat eggs in a large bowl until fluffy, approximately 2 minutes. Combine buttermilk, mashed bananas, 1/4 cup maple syrup and vegetable oil with egg mixture and set aside. In a separate bowl, combine flour, baking powder, baking soda, salt and pecans. Add liquid ingredients, stirring only until just blended.

Heat a non-stick griddle to 375°F, greasing lightly as necessary. Pour approximately 1/4 cup batter per pancake onto griddle and cook until puffed and dry around the edges, then turn and cook until golden brown. Serve pancakes with sliced bananas and strawberry halves, a dollop of "Maple caresse" cheese and drizzle with additional maple syrup. Yields 24 4-inch pancakes.

A mouth-watering breakfast, Maple Pecan Banana Pancakes are ▶ served up at Kentville's Wickwire House

VEGETABLES AND MAIN COURSES

ure maple syrup — a gift from the gods. In this section you will find many recipes using the subtle flavour of maple to infuse and enhance main course dishes. From the Quaco Inn's Baked Spaghetti Squash to the Maple Chicken from Mt. Tremblant's Château Beauvallon, there is sure to be a recipe to tempt your palate.

◀ *Carriage House Inn Salad, served with torn spinach leaves and choice of freshly shelled nuts*

CARRIAGE HOUSE INN SALAD

CARRIAGE HOUSE INN,
FREDERICTON, NB

*Joan Gorham of Fredericton's Carriage House
serves her dressing with torn spinach leaves and a
choice of freshly shelled nuts.*

1 clove garlic

2 green onions or several fresh parsley sprigs

1/3 teaspoon basil

3 tablespoons pure maple syrup

1/4 cup vinegar

1 cup canola or corn oil

prepared spinach leaves to serve 6

1/2 cup nuts (pine, almonds, walnuts or
pecans)

Place garlic, onions or parsley, basil, maple
syrup, and vinegar in a blender and process on
medium speed. Slowly add the oil in a thin,
steady stream while processing until dressing
has emulsified.

Place prepared spinach in a large salad bowl.
Toss with nuts and drizzle with dressing.
Store unused dressing refrigerated in a
tightly capped container. Yields 1 1/4 cup
salad dressing.

BAKED SPAGHETTI SQUASH

THE QUACO INN, ST. MARTINS, NB

*Spaghetti squash belongs to the tender summer
squash family. Innkeeper Betty Ann Murray says
guests at the Quaco Inn are intrigued by this
versatile vegetable.*

1/2 cup sliced almonds

1 spaghetti squash, 2 1/2–3 pounds

1/2 cup butter, melted

2 teaspoons grated orange zest

1 1/2 tablespoons fresh orange juice

1 tablespoon maple syrup

1/4 teaspoon nutmeg

Preheat oven to 325°F. Toast almonds in oven
until lightly browned, approximately 5
minutes; remove from oven and reserve.
Pierce whole spaghetti squash with a fork and
bake on a cookie sheet until tender,
approximately 1 hour. Remove from oven,
slice in half lengthwise. Scoop out and discard
seeds. Using a fork, scratch pulp from shell
and place in a bowl. Mix together almonds,
melted butter, orange zest, juice, maple syrup,
and nutmeg and pour over squash. Gently toss
to coat. Serve immediately. Serves 4–6.

MANOIR VICTORIA GRILLED CHICKEN

MANOIR VICTORIA, QUEBEC CITY, QUE

Chef Nanak Vig suggests that his marinated chicken pieces are equally delicious cooked on a barbecue grill. He serves the chicken napped with his wonderful Maple Sauce.

1 chicken, 3–4 pounds

1/2 cup vegetable oil

1/4 cup wine vinegar

1 tablespoon soya sauce

1 tablespoon finely chopped fresh ginger

2 cloves garlic, minced

1/4 cup pure maple syrup

2 tablespoons lemon juice

Manoir Victoria Maple Sauce, recipe follows

Rinse and pat dry the chicken and cut into 4–6 serving pieces. Combine remaining ingredients and marinate chicken, covered and refrigerated, for up to 24 hours. Turn chicken pieces to ensure that they are covered with marinade.

Preheat oven to 400°F. Place chicken in an ovenproof dish and bake until tender, approximately 40–45 minutes. Baste occasionally with pan juices and reserved marinade. Serve, napped with Maple Sauce. Serves 4.

Manoir Victoria Maple Sauce

1/2 cup pure maple syrup

3 tablespoons butter, at room temperature

1 tablespoon soya sauce

1 clove garlic, finely chopped

salt, pepper, and cayenne, to taste

While chicken is baking combine maple syrup, butter, soya sauce and garlic a small saucepan and bring to a boil. Reduce heat and simmer until sauce is reduced to half and thickened. Season to taste with salt, pepper, and cayenne. Yields 1/3 cup sauce.

WHISKEY AND PEACH MAPLE GLAZE

THE BRIAR INN AND COUNTRY CLUB, JACKSON'S POINT, ONT

You might want to serve this sauce with a variety of meats but the chef tells me that it is especially delicious spooned over baked or barbecued chicken breasts.

2 fresh peaches, peeled, halved, and sliced

3 tablespoons clarified butter*

2 shallots, thinly sliced

pinch of coarsely cracked black peppercorns

1/4 cup Canadian Club whiskey

1/4 cup pure maple syrup

1 1/2 tablespoons good quality balsamic vinegar

Prepare peaches and set aside. Heat clarified butter over high temperature and quickly sauté shallots and peppercorns, stirring constantly. When shallots have reached a golden colour, approximately 4 minutes, briefly remove pot from burner, add whiskey and flame. Return to heat, add peach slices and sauté until peaches are slightly softened; stir in maple syrup and cook until mixture is reduced to a thick syrup, about 7 minutes. Remove from heat and stir in balsamic vinegar. Serve warm. Yields 1–1 1/4 cups sauce.

* Clarified or drawn butter is prepared by slowly melting unsalted butter, thus evaporating most of the water and allowing the milk solids to sink to the bottom of the pan, leaving a golden liquid on the surface. Skim foam from surface, then pour or spoon the clarified butter into a container. It will take 1/4 cup of unsalted butter to make 3 tablespoons clarified butter.

WILD RICE AND MUSHROOM SOUP

PLANTERS' BARRACKS COUNTRY INN, STARRS POINT, NS

This is a delightful soup which Innkeeper Gail LeBlanc developed for her luncheon menu. She tells us that sherry can be substituted for maple syrup and that it produces an equally delicious soup.

3 cups chicken broth

1/3 cup raw wild rice, rinsed, and drained

1/2 cup thinly sliced green onions

1 cup light cream (18% m.f.)

2 tablespoons flour

1 teaspoon fresh thyme or 1/4 teaspoon dried

1/3 teaspoon pepper

1/2 cup sliced fresh mushrooms

1 tablespoon pure maple syrup

In a large saucepan combine broth and uncooked wild rice. Bring to a boil, reduce heat and simmer, covered, for 40 minutes. Stir in green onions and cook an additional 5–10 minutes until rice is tender. In a small bowl, whisk together cream, flour, thyme, and pepper. Stir cream into soup mixture and add mushrooms. Cook, stirring frequently, until soup is thickened and bubbly. Stir in maple syrup and heat through. Serves 4.

Gail LeBlanc's delightful Wild Rice and Mushroom Soup, served ▶ at the Planters' Barracks Country Inn

FRESH THYME AND MAPLE SAUCE WITH ROCK CORNISH HENS

THE BRIAR INN AND COUNTRY CLUB, JACKSON'S POINT, ONT

Executive Chef Michael Burns of Ontario's Briar Inn and Country Club developed this recipe to serve with wild rice stuffed rock Cornish hens.

Fresh Thyme and Maple Sauce

3/4 cup butter, melted

1 tablespoon fresh thyme, chopped

1 cup pure maple syrup

1/2 cup Dijon mustard

In a saucepan over low heat combine butter and chopped thyme and cook about 5 minutes. Add maple syrup and mustard; blend well. Set aside half the sauce to serve warm in a gravy boat with the Cornish hens. Yields 2 cups sauce.

Rock Cornish Hens *(supplied by author)*

6 1/2-ounce package wild rice stuffing mix (180 g)

4 rock Cornish hens, 1 pound each

salt and pepper

2 tablespoons melted butter

1 cup Fresh Thyme and Maple Sauce

Following package directions, prepare wild rice stuffing mix and set aside to cool to room temperature.

Preheat oven to 350°F. Rinse Cornish hens under cold running water and pat dry. Gently stuff hens with stuffing and truss or skewer them shut. Season with a sprinkling of salt and pepper. Place hens in a shallow baking pan, brush with melted butter and bake 3/4 hour. Remove from oven and baste with sauce. Return to oven and continue to bake, basting frequently until hens are browned and done, approximately 1/2–3/4 hour longer. Remove to a serving platter and tent with foil. Serve accompanied by warm Fresh Thyme and Maple Sauce. Serves 4.

ROAST SALMON WITH SAUTÉED FIDDLEHEADS AND MAPLE SYRUP FETTUCINI

HOTEL BEAUSEJOUR, MONCTON, NB

Chef Bettanger of Moncton's Hotel Beausejour serves his maple infused fettucini topped with an Atlantic salmon fillet and buttered New Brunswick fiddleheads.

3 cups flour

2/3 cup pure maple syrup

5 egg yolks

pinch of salt

boiling salted water for cooking

2 tablespoons butter

4 Atlantic salmon fillets, 4–6 ounces each

salt and pepper, to taste

1 lemon, juiced

3/4 lb. fresh fiddleheads, rinsed and trimmed

2 tablespoons fresh parsley, chopped

2 tablespoons butter, second amount

Prepare fettucini by combining flour, maple syrup, egg yolks, and salt. Knead on a smooth surface until mixture will form a ball. Cover with plastic wrap and refrigerate several hours.

If the dough is to be cut by hand, divide into four portions and place on a lightly floured surface. Knead for 5–10 minutes until it is silky and elastic. Roll each portion until very thin, then cut into narrow strips.

For those using a pasta machine, knead dough only briefly by hand and divide into four portions, flatten slightly and cover with plastic wrap or a cloth and let rest 1 hour. Open the smooth machine rollers fully and taking each portion of dough in turn, flour them and pass between rollers. Fold the rolled sheets into thirds, flour again and pass it through the rollers. Repeat this process 4 or 5 times, decreasing the gap between the rollers with each rolling. When dough is desired thickness, cut into noodles with the aid of the cutting rollers on the machine.

Fresh pasta can be used immediately or left to dry at room temperature until brittle, about 4 hours. The dried pasta may be stored refrigerated in a tightly covered container for 3–4 days.

To cook pasta, bring 4 quarts of water to a boil. Stir in 2 tablespoons salt and add pasta. Return to a boil, then reduce heat and simmer until *al dente*, approximately 3 minutes. Drain, toss with butter and keep warm.

At serving time, bake or poach salmon, allowing 10 minutes per inch of thickness. Season with salt, pepper and a few drops of lemon juice. While salmon is cooking, blanch fiddleheads in boiling water until crisp tender. Drain, toss with parsley and second amount of butter.

To serve, divide fettucini noodles between four serving plates. Top with salmon fillets and surround with fiddleheads. Serves 4.

MAPLE GLAZED PORK LOIN

THE BRIAR INN AND COUNTRY CLUB,
JACKSON'S POINT, ONT

Have your butcher trim, debone, and tie the pork loin into a uniform shape. It is no longer necessary to over-cook pork. Your roast will be tender and juicy when a meat thermometer registers around 165–170°F.

Boneless pork loin, approximately 4 pounds

salt and pepper

1 tablespoon each chopped fresh oregano, thyme, and marjoram

1/3 cup pommery seed mustard

1/2–3/4 cup pure maple syrup

1/2 cup white wine

Preheat oven to 375°F. Score the fat side of the roast into the meat. Season with salt and pepper, then rub the herbs into the scoring cuts. Coat the roast with mustard and bake on a rack about 20 minutes. Reduce oven temperature to 350°F. Remove pan from oven and drizzle top of roast with a little maple syrup, being careful not to spill the syrup onto the hot roasting pan. Continue to bake, drizzling with additional syrup until roast is cooked, approximately 2 hours. Remove roast from pan, tent with foil and keep warm. Place roasting pan over a burner, add wine and simmer the drippings until thickened. Add more maple syrup, if desired. To serve, thinly slice pork and top with sauce. Serves 4–6.

NOVA SCOTIA MAPLE SYRUP BAKED BEANS

LISCOMBE LODGE,
LISCOMB MILLS, NS

At Liscombe Lodge the chef serves his maple infused baked beans with his breakfast menu. I think you will enjoy the delicate flavour of his rendition of baked beans.

1 pound dry white beans, rinsed and cleaned

6 cups water

6 slices bacon, cut in 2-inch pieces

1 small onion, chopped

1/2 teaspoon dry mustard

1 1/2 teaspoons salt

1/2 cup dark maple syrup

2 tablespoons brown sugar

2 tablespoons butter

Bring the beans and water to a boil in a large saucepan and boil for 2 minutes. Remove from heat and let stand, covered, for an hour. Return to a boil, reduce heat and simmer, covered, for 40 minutes. Drain, reserving cooking liquid.

Place half of the bacon in a bean crock, add beans. In a separate bowl combine the reserved cooking liquid, onion, dry mustard, salt and maple syrup. Pour over the beans and top with remaining bacon. Bake, covered at 325°F for about 3 hours, checking occasionally and adding a bit of water if beans appear dry.

Cream together the brown sugar and butter. Sprinkle over the beans and bake, uncovered, an additional hour. Serves 6–8.

*Liscombe Lodge's Nova Scotia Maple Syrup Baked Beans ▶
are infused with delicate flavour*

LAKE BROME DUCKLING BRAISED IN MAPLE SYRUP SAUCE

AUX ANCIENS CANADIENS, QUEBEC CITY, QUE

Chef Dominique Nourry debones his duck cutlets and removes all skin, thus eliminating much of the grease that normally accompanies the meat. He serves his cutlets napped with the maple syrup sauce accompanied by rice and seasonal vegetables.

4 duck cutlets, deboned and skin removed

vegetable oil for browning

Maple Syrup Sauce, recipe follows

Preheat oven to 350°F. Prepare duck cutlets and sear in a lightly greased skillet, turning once. Remove duck to an ovenproof baking dish and roast for approximately 10 minutes or until duck is lightly pink in the centre. Serve duck cutlets, napped with Maple Syrup Sauce. Serves 4.

Maple Syrup Sauce

The chef at Aux Anciens Canadiens prepares demi-glace in the classic manner by reducing stock, maple syrup and lemon zest. What follows is a simplified version.

1 package Knorr demi-glace

3/4 cup cold water

1/2 cup pure maple syrup

1 teaspoon chocolate syrup

1/2 teaspoon lemon zest, blanched

In a saucepan stir demi-glace mix with cold water and maple syrup. Bring to a boil over medium-high heat, stirring frequently with a whisk. Add chocolate syrup and lemon zest, reduce heat and simmer 3 minutes, stirring occasionally. Strain and serve.

◄ *Deboned cutlets make Lake Brome Duckling Braised in Maple Syrup Sauce a wise choice for the selective diner*

SUGARBUSH INN'S HAZELNUT CRUSTED CHICKEN

SUGARBUSH INN, WARREN, VT

Steve Ogden, executive chef at the Sugarbush Inn serves chicken breasts accompanied by a tangy Apricot Compote and topped with a Brandied Maple Glaze.

4 chicken breasts, boneless and skinless, about 5 ounces each

8 ounces hazelnuts

1 cup flour

1/4 cup dry breadcrumbs

1 large egg, beaten

2 tablespoons butter

fresh herb sprigs, as garnish

Apricot Compote

4 fresh apricots, peeled and seeded

1/3 cup canned apricot or pineapple juice

1/3 cup apricot preserves

1/3 cup brandy

2 tablespoons brown sugar

Brandied Maple Glaze

1/2 cup pure maple syrup

1/4 cup brandy

Preheat oven to 350°F. Trim chicken breasts of any bits of fat, rinse and pat dry. Combine hazelnuts, 1/2 cup flour and breadcrumbs in a food processor and process until mixture is fine in texture. Beat egg and place in a small shallow bowl. In a second bowl, place remaining 1/2 cup flour. In a third bowl place hazelnut mixture. Dredge chicken first in flour, then egg wash and finally in hazelnut mixture. Refrigerate chicken while you prepare the Apricot Compote.

Combine all compote ingredients in a large saucepan and cook over low heat until mixture thickens and fruit is soft. Keep warm.

Combine maple syrup and brandy in a saucepan and warm, being careful not to boil. Set aside.

To serve, melt butter in a skillet over medium heat and sear chicken until golden brown on both sides. Transfer to oven and bake approximately 20 minutes until chicken is cooked and no longer pink inside. Place a bed of warm compote on serving plate, top with chicken and drizzle with Maple Glaze. Garnish with fresh herb sprigs. Serves 4.

MAPLE CHICKEN

CHÂTEAU BEAUVALLON, MT. TREMBLANT, QUE

Mt. Tremblant innkeepers Alex and Judy Riddell serve traditional French Canadian dishes using local ingredients. I feel their Maple Chicken reflects the best of Quebecois cuisine.

1 chicken (3 1/2–4 pounds)

salt and pepper, to season

1 tablespoon vegetable oil

2 tablespoons diced celery

2 tablespoons diced carrot

1 1/2 tablespoons minced leek, white part only

1/4 cup pure maple syrup

1/3 cup cider vinegar

1 cup chicken stock

1 1/2 tablespoons pure maple syrup (second amount)

1 tablespoon butter

1 tablespoon flour

Preheat oven to 450°F. Rinse and pat dry chicken, season cavity with salt and pepper and rub skin with oil. Roast, breast side up, in an open roasting pan, for 10 minutes. Reduce heat to 350°F. and continue to bake for about 30 minutes.

Add celery, carrot, leek, and 1/4 cup maple syrup to pan juices. Baste and continue to bake another 30 minutes. Stir in vinegar and baste again. Continue to bake and baste until meat is tender and a thermometer inserted into the thickest part of the thigh, not touching bone, reaches an internal temperature of 185°F. Remove chicken to a heated platter and tent with foil.

Place roasting pan over medium heat and stir in chicken stock and 1 1/2 tablespoons maple syrup, bring to a simmer. Cream together the butter and flour to form *beurre manié* and add to sauce, stirring until lightly thickened. Strain sauce.

To serve, brush chicken with a little sauce, return to a 500°F oven and glaze several minutes. Serve remaining sauce in a separate bowl at tableside. Serves 4.

ALGONQUIN MAPLE SYRUP AND MUSTARD BARBECUED LAMB CHOPS

ALGONQUIN HOTEL, ST. ANDREWS, NB

Executive Chef Willie White prepares his marinade a day in advance to allow the flavours to blend. He experiments by adding more garlic and ginger for a stronger flavour or chopped chili peppers for spice! While in this presentation it is served with grilled lamb chops, he tells me that this is a multi-purpose marinade and will also complement chicken, pork or beef.

1/2 cup pure maple syrup

3 teaspoons Dijon-style grained mustard

zest and juice of 1 fresh lemon

4 teaspoons balsamic vinegar

4–6 twists of freshly grated pepper

1 garlic clove, finely chopped

1 teaspoon finely grated fresh ginger

1/4 cup canola oil

12 rib lamb chops, 2–3 ounces each

Blend together all ingredients, except the lamb chops. Refrigerate, covered for 24 hours.

Marinate the meat, refrigerated, for 45 minutes then barbecue over low to medium heat until meat is browned on the outside and pink on the inside. Brush with marinade while grilling to keep meat moist. Serves 4.

Mustard Barbecqued Lamb Chops with a multi-purpose marinade ▶
that also complements other meat dishes

MAPLE GLAZED HAM

LOON BAY LODGE, ST. STEPHEN, NB

Loon Bay Lodge is located in a pristine setting beside the international St. Croix River. They serve this delicious baked ham accompanied by scalloped potatoes and fresh garden vegetables.

1 ham, uncooked (4–6 pounds)

1/2 cup water

1/4 cup pure maple syrup

1/4 cup table syrup

1 teaspoon soya sauce

1 1/2 teaspoons cornstarch

1–2 tablespoons cold water

granulated maple sugar to garnish

Preheat oven to 350°F. Place ham on a rack in a large roasting pan and add 1/2 cup water. Cover with foil and bake, allowing 25 minutes per pound of meat.

During last half hour of baking time prepare glaze. Combine maple syrup, table syrup, and soya sauce together in a small saucepan and bring to a boil. Combine cornstarch and cold water and add enough cornstarch mixture to boiling sauce to thicken slightly.

Remove ham from oven and trim away fatty layer on outside of roast.

Score meat in a diamond pattern, reduce oven temperature to 325°F. Pour maple glaze over ham and bake, uncovered an additional 20 minutes. Insert a meat thermometer into the thickest part of the ham, being careful not to touch any bone. The ham is cooked when its internal temperature reaches 160°F.

Remove from oven and allow to stand, tented with foil, for approximately 5 minutes before carving. Serves 6–8.

◄ *The Maple Glazed Ham at Loon Bay Lodge is served up with scalloped potatoes and fresh garden vegetables*

PAN ROASTED PORK TENDERLOIN

SEASONS IN THYME, SUMMERSIDE, PEI

Stefan Czapalay, owner/chef of Seasons in Thyme prepares imaginative dishes using fruits and vegetables of the season. With the wonderful blend of apple cider and maple syrup, this will surely become a favourite.

2 pork tenderloins, 10–12 ounces each

2 teaspoons canola oil

2–3 tablespoons finely diced sweet potatoes

1 teaspoon diced fresh ginger

1/4 cup pecan halves

1 Anjou pear, thinly sliced

1/2 cup apple cider or juice

1/2 cup maple syrup

1 teaspoons balsamic or cider vinegar

1 teaspoons brown sugar

Preheat oven to 350°F. Trim tenderloins of any fat and sliver skin, slice into medallions. Heat oil in a heavy bottomed saucepan and sauté medallions until golden brown, turning once. Finish cooking pork in oven for approximately 5 minutes.

While pork is baking, prepare sauce. Add potatoes, ginger, and pecans to saucepan and sauté for 1 minute. Add cider or juice and vinegar, reduce heat slightly. Add maple syrup, brown sugar, and pear slices and cook until reduced to a thick syrup.

To serve, divide pork medallions and pear slices between serving plates and nap with maple sauce. Serves 4–6.

Pan Roasted Pork Tenderloin is just one of chef Stefan ▶
Czapalay's imaginative dishes

DESSERTS

There are two types of cookbook fanatics. The first looks at the main course selections, and the second rushes to the desserts. If sweets are your thing, then the maple syrup desserts that follow are all you will ever need to complete your dinner.

◄ *Maple Meringues with Peaches are a delicious choice at the Falcourt Inn in Nictaux, NS*

FALCOURT INN'S MAPLE MERINGUES WITH PEACHES

FALCOURT INN, NICTAUX, NS

Meringues will keep for up to a week if stored in an airtight container. They are easy to prepare and are the basis of many stunning desserts.

4 egg whites, at room temperature

pinch of salt

1/4 teaspoon cream of tartar

1/4 cup pure maple syrup

drop of vanilla

2 tablespoons pure maple syrup (2nd amount)

16 fresh or canned peach slices

rich vanilla ice cream (optional)

Preheat oven to 250°F. In a large bowl, beat egg whites, salt, and cream of tartar until soft peaks form. Slowly add 1/4 cup maple syrup and vanilla and continue to beat until stiff glossy peaks form. Pipe or spoon onto a parchment paper lined baking sheet, forming small rounds. Place in oven and bake approximately 1 hour, turn off heat and leave meringues in oven until cooled to room temperature. Remove and store in an airtight container up to 1 week. Yields 10–12 meringues.

Marinate peach slices in second amount maple syrup for at least one hour. To serve, place meringue in centre of dessert plate; surround with peach slices. With a melon baller, scoop out three small scoops of ice cream per dessert and place between peach slices. Serves 4–6.

PARKER'S LODGE MAPLE SYRUP SQUARES

THE PARKER'S LODGE, VAL-DAVID, QUE

Guaranteed to satisfy the most discriminating sweet tooth, these squares are easy to prepare and oh, so delicious.

Base
1/2 cup butter

1/4 cup brown sugar

1 cup flour

Topping

2/3 cup brown sugar, firmly packed

2 eggs, beaten

1/4 teaspoon salt

1 cup walnuts or pecans, chopped

1 cup pure maple syrup

2 tablespoons flour

1 teaspoon vanilla

Preheat oven to 350°F. In a food processor or mixing bowl, combine butter, brown sugar, and flour and mix well. Press into a greased, floured 8-inch square baking pan; bake 15 minutes.

In a large bowl combine topping ingredients and pour over base. Return to oven and bake an additional 30 minutes or until topping is browned and bubbly. Cool and cut into squares.

PECAN AND SWEET POTATO PIE WITH MUSKOKA MAPLE SYRUP

GRANDVIEW INN, HUNTSVILLE, ONT

At the Grandview Inn, in Ontario's beautiful Muskoka region, they produce most of their own maple syrup. Their guests can enjoy a naturalist program during the maple syrup run, and observe the evolution of maple syrup production from native to modern methods.

Sweet Dough

3 tablespoons unsalted butter, softened

2 tablespoons sugar

1/4 teaspoon salt

1 egg, beaten

2 tablespoons cold milk

1 cup flour

Using an electric mixer, beat together the butter, sugar and salt until mixture is creamy. In a small bowl, whisk egg until frothy. Add half of egg and milk to butter mixture, and beat 2 minutes longer. Fold in flour until just fully incorporated, being careful not to overmix. Wrap dough in plastic wrap and chill 1 hour.

Roll out dough on a lightly floured surface and line a 10-inch pie plate.

Filling

1 cup cooked sweet potato pulp (approximately 2–3 sweet potatoes)

1/4 cup light brown sugar, packed

2 tablespoons white sugar

1/2 egg from dough recipe

3 tablespoons heavy cream (35% m.f.)

1 tablespoon unsalted butter

1 tablespoon vanilla

1/4 teaspoon salt

1/4 teaspoon cinnamon

1/8 teaspoon nutmeg

1 cup pure maple syrup

1/2 cup evaporated milk

2 eggs

1 1/2 tablespoons unsalted butter, melted

2 teaspoons vanilla, second amount

pinch salt

pinch cinnamon

1 cup pecan halves

Preheat oven to 425°F. Combine sweet potatoes, brown and white sugars, remaining egg from dough recipe, heavy cream, butter, vanilla, salt, cinnamon, and nutmeg and beat together until smooth. In a separate bowl combine maple syrup, evaporated milk, eggs, melted butter, vanilla, salt, and cinnamon. Fold maple syrup mixture into sweet potato mixture and pour into prepared pie shell. Bake 10 minutes, reduce oven temperature to 350°F and continue to bake until a knife inserted in the centre of the pie comes out clean (approximately 45 minutes). Remove from oven and decorate with pecan halves. Serves 8.

LISCOMBE LODGE MAPLE SYRUP CREAM

LISCOMBE LODGE,
LISCOMB MILLS, NS

This simple, elegant dessert makes a beautiful presentation served in stemmed glasses, decorated with fresh berries and mint leaves.

1 tablespoon gelatin

1/4 cup cold water

1/2 cup milk, scalded

2/3 cup pure maple syrup

1/8 teaspoon salt

2 cups heavy cream (35% m.f.), whipped

Fresh fruit and mint leaves as garnish

Soak gelatin in cold water for 5 minutes, then stir into scalded milk. Add maple syrup and salt and chill until mixture begins to thicken, approximately 45 minutes. Prepare whipped cream and gently fold into gelatin mixture. Pour into a large bowl or six individual serving dishes. Chill several hours, until firm. Garnish with fruit and mint leaves, if desired. Serves 6.

MAPLE SYRUP COMPOTE

FALCOURT INN, NICTAUX, NS

This is a simple dish to prepare. In fact, chef Brian Veinott serves this fresh fruit compote with continental breakfast or as an evening dessert.

2 oranges, peeled, seeded, and cubed

1 small cantaloupe, peeled, and cubed

2 bananas, sliced

1/2 pound seedless grapes, sliced

1 cup honeydew melon balls

1 cup pure maple syrup

mint leaves, as garnish

Place all ingredients in a bowl and let stand, refrigerated, overnight. Serve in individual dessert dishes, garnished with mint leaves, if desired. Serves 6–8.

Chef Brian Veinott serves Maple Syrup Compote with continental ▶
breakfast and as an evening dessert

CINNAMON MAPLE APPLES WITH CARAMEL

INN AT THORN HILL, JACKSON, NH

Ibby Cooper, innkeeper at the Inn at Thorn Hill calls this wonderful dessert an "indulgence, but worth it." I think you will agree!

8 small Golden Delicious or McIntosh apples

9 tablespoons pure maple syrup

6 tablespoons butter

2 teaspoons cinnamon, divided

2 packages frozen puff pastry, thawed

1 large egg

1 tablespoon sugar

Caramel Sauce

6 tablespoons butter

1/2 cup firmly packed brown sugar

1/2 cup light corn syrup

1/2 cup heavy cream (35% m.f.)

1 1/2 teaspoons vanilla

Line a large cookie sheet with foil and grease lightly. Cut a 1-inch wide strip of peel around the centre of each apple, trim bottoms to allow them to stand upright. Carefully remove 3/4 of the core from each apple, being careful not to cut through the bottom. Arrange apples on prepared foil.

Combine maple syrup, butter and 1 1/2 teaspoons cinnamon in a small saucepan. Cook over medium heat until butter melts, then divide mixture between apple cavities. Refrigerate apples for 15 minutes.

While apples are chilling, roll each pastry sheet on a floured surface into a 12-inch square. Cut pastry into a 6 x 8-inch rectangle and place an apple in the centre of each rectangle. Brush pastry edges with water and pull up corners, gathering and pinching pastry along the seams, until all apples have been encased. Return apples to cookie sheet and refrigerate 1 hour.

Heat oven to 450°F. Lightly beat egg and 1 teaspoon water in a cup. Combine sugar and remaining 1/2 teaspoon cinnamon. Line a jelly-roll pan with foil and lightly grease. Before baking, brush with egg wash, prick pastry and sprinkle with cinnamon sugar. Bake 18 minutes until pastry is golden. Serve immediately with Caramel Sauce. Serves 8.

Caramel Sauce

Combine butter, sugar and corn syrup in a medium saucepan. Simmer over medium low heat, stirring occasionally until mixture darkens and thickens, approximately 10–15 minutes. Carefully stir in heavy cream and vanilla until smooth. Serve warm. Yields 1 1/2 cups sauce.

MAPLE SYRUP GINGERBREAD

LISCOMBE LODGE,
LISCOMB MILLS, NS

Warm from the oven, this old time favourite takes on a new flavour with the addition of maple syrup.

1 1/3 cups flour

1 teaspoon baking powder

1 teaspoon ginger

1/2 teaspoon soda

1/2 teaspoon salt

3/4 cup pure maple syrup

1/2 cup vegetable oil

1 egg, beaten

1/3 cup warm water

Preheat oven to 350°F. Grease and flour an 8-inch baking pan.

Mix together the dry ingredients in a large bowl. In a separate bowl, combine maple syrup, oil, and egg, beating until smooth; blend in warm water. Make a well in the dry ingredients and add the syrup mixture, stirring until flour mixture is moistened. Pour into prepared pan and bake 30 minutes or until cake springs back in the centre when lightly touched. Serves 6–8.

MAPLE SYRUP CREAM

THE PRINCE EDWARD HOTEL,
CHARLOTTETOWN, PEI

Chef Joerg Soltermann of Charlottetown's Prince Edward Hotel uses this simple Maple Syrup Cream to enhance apple pie, fresh berries, ice cream or any dessert you may choose!

1 cup heavy cream (35% m.f.)

3 1/2 tablespoons pure maple syrup

Combine above ingredients in a saucepan and bring to a simmer. Refrigerate immediately and when cool, whip like whipping cream.

DUNDEE MAPLE BUTTER TART WITH MARITIME MAPLE SAUCE

THE DUNDEE ARMS, CHARLOTTETOWN, PEI

Maple flavour at its best, at the Dundee Arms the chef decorates his plate using a real maple leaf for a spectacular presentation.

Pastry

1 1/4 cups flour

pinch of salt

1/2 cup shortening

2–3 tablespoons ice water to bind

Filling

1/3 cup butter

1/3 cup pure maple syrup

1/2 teaspoon vanilla

1 cup brown sugar

pinch of salt

2 eggs

Sauce

2 egg yolks

2/3 cup pure maple syrup

1/4 cup brown sugar

1/2 cup heavy cream (35% m.f.), whipped

1/4 cup heavy cream (35% m.f.), unwhipped

Combine flour and salt in a mixing bowl. Cut in shortening with a pastry blender until mixture is the size of large peas. Do not overmix. Sprinkle ice water over mixture and blend with a fork until absorbed. Form into a ball and roll out on a floured surface. Cut into eight 3 1/2-inch rounds and place in muffin tins. Set aside.

Preheat oven to 375°F. Prepare filling by melting butter in a saucepan over medium heat. Add syrup, vanilla, brown sugar, and salt; mix well. Beat eggs in a separate bowl and add to mixture. Fill pastries and bake approximately 15 minutes, until tarts are browned and filling is bubbly. Remove from oven and set aside 10 minutes.

While pastries are baking, prepare sauce. In a double boiler, over simmering but not boiling water, heat egg yolks, maple syrup and sugar until mixture thickens and coats the back of a spoon. Cool over ice cubes, stirring constantly. Fold in whipped cream, then fold in unwhipped cream. Refrigerate.

To serve, spread a little sauce on a dessert plate and top with tart. Serves 8.

◄ *Elegantly presented Dundee Maple Butter Tart with Maritime Maple Sauce*

APPLE TARTE TATIN WITH MAPLE AND DRIED FRUIT CHIPS

UNNI'S RESTAURANT, HALIFAX, NS

This is a wonderful wintertime dessert. Restaurateur Unni Simensen serves her dessert accompanied by Crème Fraîche and dried fruit chips.

1 1/4 cups pure maple syrup

1 cup plus 1 tablespoon heavy cream (35% m.f.)

1/3 cup unsalted butter

6 Granny Smith apples, peeled, cored, and sliced

1 package frozen puff pastry, thawed in refrigerator

good quality vanilla ice cream

1 cup Crème Fraîche, recipe follows

fresh mint, for garnish

Fruit Chips, recipe follows

Preheat oven to 400°F. In a saucepan, over medium heat, combine maple syrup and heavy cream. Bring to a boil then lower heat and reduce by 20%. Stir in butter and bring back to a boil, continue cooking for 4–5 minutes. Remove from burner and divide between 6 individual small soufflé baking dishes.

Peel and core apples, then slice into wedges. Place apple slices on top of sauce in baking dishes. Roll out puff pastry until it is 1/4 inch thick. Cut into rounds to cover ceramic dishes and bake 25–30 minutes, until pastry is puffed and browned. Invert onto dessert plates, top with ice cream and garnish with Crème Fraîche, fresh mint and Dried Fruit Chips. Serves 6.

Crème Fraîche *(supplied by author)*

Crème Fraîche is a mature thickened cream that is easy to prepare and will keep refrigerated for up to one week. Simply place 1 cup heavy cream (35% m.f.) in a glass bowl, stir in 2 tablespoons buttermilk and cover. Allow to stand at room temperature, approximately 70°F for 8–24 hours. Stir well, cover and refrigerate.

Fruit Chips

Preheat oven to 200°F. Slice an assortment of fresh fruit very thin and place on a parchment paper cover baking sheet. Dust with icing sugar and dry in oven several hours.

Apple Tarte Tatin with Maple and Dried Fruit Chips is a wonderful wintertime treat ▲

"GRAND-PÈRES" AU SIROP D'ÉRABLE

THE PARKER'S LODGE,
VAL-DAVID, QUE

A dumpling with a difference — this is a simple to prepare dessert, but oh, so good. Chef Rollande Thisdele at the Parker's Lodge serves this dessert warm, in individual serving dishes with a generous dollop of whipped cream.

1 cup pure maple syrup

1 cup water

1 cup flour

1/2 teaspoon salt

2 teaspoons baking powder

1 tablespoon butter

1/2 cup milk

1/2 cup heavy cream (35% m.f.), whipped

In a deep pot bring maple syrup and water to a boil. In a bowl, whisk together flour, salt, and baking powder. Cut in butter with a pastry blender and stir in milk to make a soft dough. Drop the batter by spoonfuls on top of the simmering maple sauce. Immediately cover saucepan and cook over medium heat without removing cover for 15–18 minutes. Serve dumplings and syrup warm, with a dollop of whipped cream. Serves 4–6.

VERMONT MAPLE CRÈME BRÛLÉE

SUGARBUSH INN, WARREN, VT

This is an excellent dessert that can be prepared early in the day and placed under the broiler just at serving time.

9 egg yolks

4 cups heavy cream (35% m.f.)

1/2 cup pure maple syrup

2 1/2 tablespoons single malt scotch whiskey

brown sugar for sprinkling

Preheat oven to 350°F. In a large bowl mix egg yolks, cream, syrup, and scotch until blended. Warm over low heat in a saucepan but do not scald mixture or allow to boil. Strain mixture and divide between 8 large custard cups.

Place custard cups in a large roasting pan. Pour water to 1–inch depth into the pan. Bake until custard is set, approximately 30–40 minutes. Remove cups from water bath and refrigerate until ready to serve.

At serving time sprinkle each dessert with a thin layer of brown sugar. Place under a broiler until golden brown. Serve immediately. Serves 8.

BLUEBERRY MAPLE CHIFFON CONES

CATHERINE McKINNON'S SPOT O' TEA, STANLEY BRIDGE, PEI

Pastry Chef Whitney Armstrong prepares her cones and maple chiffon early in the day. I caution that the batter tends to spread, thus you should allow only 3 or 4 cones per cookie sheet. The method of forming the cones is easily achieved if you have metal "cream horn molds". She accompanies her dessert with fresh blueberries when available.

Tulip Cones

7 tablespoons butter, softened

1 cup icing sugar

7 tablespoons egg whites

1/2 cup flour

Preheat oven to 350°F. With an electric mixer, combine butter, icing sugar, egg whites and flour. Line two baking sheets with foil and liberally spray with no-stick cooking oil. Allowing approximately 2 tablespoons of dough per cone, spread out on the foil in a circle and bake only until the dough is brown on the edges. Remove from oven and quickly shape into cones using metal cream horn molds, if available; then cool.

Maple Chiffon

4 eggs

1/2 cup pure maple syrup

1/2 cup sugar

1 tablespoon lemon juice

1 tablespoon powdered gelatin

1/4 cup hot water

2 cups heavy cream (35% m.f.), whipped

1/2–3/4 cup fresh blueberries

additional maple syrup for garnish

In the top half of a double boiler, over medium heat, whisk together eggs, maple syrup, sugar, and lemon juice until thick and frothy. Combine gelatin and hot water and whisk into egg-syrup mixture.

Remove from heat and whisk over ice cubes, until cool. Fold in whipped cream and refrigerate several hours.

To serve, pipe maple chiffon into cones, garnish with fresh blueberries and a drizzle of maple syrup. Serves 4–6.

Blueberry and Maple Chiffon Cones are a colourful and tasty choice ▶
at Catherine McKinnon's Spot O' Tea in Stanley Bridge, PEI

ACADIAN APPLE PIE

HOTEL BEAUSEJOUR, MONCTON, NB

Chef Denis Bettinger of Moncton's Hotel Beausejour provided the recipe for this delicious and decadent dessert.

1/2 cup raisins

3/4 cup apple juice

1/3 cup water

1/2 cup sugar

4 medium-large apples, peeled and sliced

1/4 teaspoon salt

1 teaspoon grated lemon zest

1/2 teaspoon lemon juice

1 tablespoon butter

1/4 teaspoon cinnamon

2 tablespoons cornstarch

1/3 cup cold water

3/4 cup walnut pieces

9-inch pie plate lined with Sweet Dough (recipe follows)

1/4 cup melted butter

1/2 cup sugar

1/2 cup flour

1/2 cup rolled oats

1/4 cup pure maple syrup for topping

Rinse and dry raisins. In a saucepan, combine raisins, apple juice, 1/3 cup water, sugar, apples, salt, lemon zest and juice, 1 tablespoon butter and cinnamon. Bring to a boil, reduce heat and simmer over medium heat for 5 minutes. Dissolve cornstarch in 1/3 cup cold water and stir into raisin mixture. Bring to a boil, then simmer three minutes. Remove from heat and stir in walnuts. Spoon mixture into prepared pie plate which has been lined with Sweet Dough.

Preheat oven to 350°F. Mix together melted butter, 1/2 cup sugar, flour and oats and sprinkle over pie. Bake 35–45 minutes until lightly browned. Serve warm or chilled, drizzled with maple syrup.

Sweet Dough

1/3 cup sugar

1/3 cup butter, softened

1 small egg, beaten

1 cup flour

With a mixer, whip sugar and butter until light and fluffy. Add egg and continue to beat. Mix in flour and form into a ball. Roll the dough on a floured surface to fit into a shallow 9-inch pie plate.

MAPLE APPLE COFFEE CAKE

INN ON THE LAKE, WAVERLEY, NS

Chef Helmut Pflueger combines the wonderful flavours of tart Nova Scotia apples and pure maple syrup in his rendition of coffee cake.

8 tablespoons butter, softened

3 eggs

1/2 cup pure maple syrup

2 teaspoons vanilla

2 cups flour

2 teaspoons baking powder

1/8 teaspoon salt

1 teaspoon cinnamon

Topping

3 large tart apples, peeled, cored, and sliced

1/4 teaspoon freshly ground nutmeg

4 tablespoons sugar

1/2 teaspoon cinnamon, second amount

2 tablespoons butter, softened

Preheat oven to 375°F and butter a 9-inch round cake pan. Beat butter with an electric mixer until light and fluffy. Add eggs one at a time, beating well after each addition. Add maple syrup and vanilla and continue to beat until mixture is fully combined.

In a separate bowl, sift together flour, baking powder, salt, cinnamon, and nutmeg. Fold dry ingredients into butter mixture and spoon the batter into the prepared pan.

Prepare topping by tossing apples with nutmeg, sugar, cinnamon and butter. Arrange decoratively on top of batter and bake 50–60 minutes until the apples are tender and a toothpick inserted in the centre of the cake comes out clean. Remove to a wire rack and allow to cool 10 minutes before removing from the pan. Serve warm, sliced in wedges. Serves 8.

Chef Helmut Pflueger's Maple Apple Coffee Cakes, Inn on the Lake, Waverley, NS ▼

MAPLE SYRUP PIE

AUX ANCIENS CANADIENS, QUEBEC CITY, QUE

Dominique Nourry of Quebec City's Aux Anciens Canadiens restaurant serves this traditional pie accompanied by a spoonful of whipped cream.

1 1/2 cups brown sugar

1/2 cup heavy cream (35% m.f.)

1/3 cup pure maple syrup

1 large egg, at room temperature

2 teaspoons butter, at room temperature

8-inch prebaked pie shell

whipped cream, as garnish

Preheat oven to 350°F. In a large bowl with an electric mixer blend together sugar, cream, maple syrup, egg, and butter until smooth and creamy. Pour into prepared pie shell and bake 45 minutes. Remove from oven and cool to room temperature. Serve garnished with freshly whipped cream. Serves 6.

Dominique Nourry's traditional Maple Syrup Pie comes ▶
with a spoonful of whipped cream

CHÂTEAU BONNE ENTENTE MAPLE AND APPLE CRÊPES

CHÂTEAU BONNE ENTENTE, SAINTE FOY, QUE

While the chef at Château Bonne Entente included a crêpe or pancake recipe, he advises that commercially prepared crêpes will work as well.

Crêpes

1 1/2 cups flour

1/4 cup sugar

pinch salt

3 eggs, beaten

2 cups milk

2 teaspoons butter, melted

1 tablespoon butter, second amount

In a large bowl, mix together the flour, sugar, and salt. Combine eggs, milk, and melted butter in a separate bowl and add to flour mixture stirring only until blended. Allow batter to rest 2–3 hours.

Heat a crêpe or omelet pan over moderate heat and melt 1 tablespoon butter. Spoon in approximately 2 tablespoons of batter, tipping the skillet to spread it. When lightly browned, flip crêpe and brown other side. Repeat this procedure until all the batter has been used, adding a little more butter when necessary. Set aside to cool.

Filling

4 apples, peeled, cored, and sliced

1/4 cup butter

2 tablespoons cornstarch dissolved in a little cold water

1 cup pure maple syrup

1 teaspoon vanilla

Sauce

1 cup heavy cream (35% m.f.)

1/3 cup brown sugar

1 teaspoon vanilla

Combine apple slices in a saucepan with melted butter and cook over medium heat approximately 3 minutes, stirring occasionally. Remove pan from burner. Dissolve cornstarch and stir into maple syrup, add vanilla. Combine apples and syrup mixture and return to burner, cooking only until apples are tender and sauce has thickened. Set aside.

In a small saucepan over medium heat bring cream and brown sugar to a boil. Reduce heat and simmer 5 minutes. Remove from heat and stir in vanilla.

Preheat oven to 325°F. Place 2 tablespoons apple mixture on each crêpe and roll. Place crêpes on a buttered ovenproof pan, drizzle with sauce, cover with aluminum foil and bake 10 minutes. Serve warm.

Maple and Apple Crêpes, from the Château Bonne Entente in Sainte Foy, Que ▶

FRESH FRUIT IN BRANDY MAPLE CREAM

BLUENOSE LODGE, LUNENBURG, NS

Grace Swan of Lunenburg's Bluenose Lodge tells me that this is the easiest recipe in her repertoire, and one of her guests' favourites.

2 cups fresh fruit (raspberries, kiwi, peach slices, etc.)

3 tablespoons light sour cream

1 tablespoon pure maple syrup

1 teaspoon brandy

Divide fruit between four serving dishes. In a small bowl whisk together the sour cream, maple syrup and brandy. Drizzle over fruit and serve immediately. Serves 4.

MAPLE PARFAIT

THE PALLISER RESTAURANT, TRURO, NS

Keltie Bruce of the Palliser relays the story that as a child she refused to eat Christmas pudding. Her mother developed this recipe and served it only for the holidays, thus they affectionately call it "Maple Christmas." At the restaurant they serve these elegant parfaits with a teaspoon of crème de cacao, a dollop of whipped cream, and chocolate sprinkles.

1/2 cup pure maple syrup

2 eggs, at room temperature

1 cup heavy cream (35% m.f.)

crème de cacao, whipped cream and chocolate sprinkles for garnish

In a small saucepan heat maple syrup almost to a boil. Remove from heat and place in a mixing bowl. Add eggs and beat on medium high speed until mixture is fully blended, approximately 5 minutes. Refrigerate several hours until well chilled.

Whip heavy cream until stiff peaks form, then using an electric mixer, beat into maple mixture. Pour into parfait glasses, cover with plastic wrap and freeze. Remove from freezer 10 minutes before serving. Serves 6–8.

Keltie Bruce's Maple Parfait, served with crème de cacao, ▶ whipped cream, and chocolate sprinkles

TARTE AU FONDANT À L'ÉRABLE

CHÂTEAU BONNE ENTENTE, SAINTE FOY, QUE

Quebec pure maple syrup is an intrinsic ingredient at the restaurant of Château Bonne Entente. I'm sure after you try this delicious pie, the recipe will become a family favourite.

2 cups graham cracker crumbs

1/3 cup pure maple syrup

1/3 cup butter, melted

1/4 cup butter, second amount

1 cup caramels, preferably maple flavoured (30-32)

1 cup 2% milk, warmed

3 large egg yolks

1 envelope unflavoured gelatin

3 tablespoons cold water

1/4 cup boiling water

1/2 cup heavy cream (35% m.f.)

3 tablespoons pure maple syrup

Preheat oven to 375°F. Prepare crust by mixing together graham cracker crumbs, 1/3 cup maple syrup and melted butter. Pat into a lightly greased 9-inch pie plate and bake 8 minutes. Remove from oven and set aside to cool.

Over boiling water in a double boiler combine second amount of butter, caramels, and warm milk. Cook, stirring constantly, until caramels are melted and mixture comes to a boil. Remove from stove and immediately whisk in egg yolks, stirring until fully incorporated. Sprinkle gelatin over cold water and allow to soften, approximately 5 minutes. Stir boiling water into gelatin, then fold into caramel mixture. Pour into prepared crust, cover with plastic wrap and refrigerate until firm, approximately 3–4 hours.

At serving time, whip heavy cream until soft peaks form. Gently whip in 3 tablespons maple syrup and continue to beat until cream stiffens. Cut pie in wedges and serve with a dollop of maple flavoured whipped cream. Serves 6–8.

Tarte au Fondant À L'Érable is sure to become a family favourite ▶

INDEX